Coping
with
Sleep Issues
workbook

Facilitator Reproducible
Guided Self-Exploration
Activities

Ester R.A. Leutenberg
& John J. Liptak, EdD

WholePerson
Mental Health & Wellness
publisher of therapy, counseling, and self-help resources
Duluth, Minnesota

WholePerson
Mental Health & Wellness
publisher of therapy, counseling, and self-help resources

101 West 2nd Street, Suite 203
Duluth, MN 55802

800-247-6789

Books@WholePerson.com
WholePerson.com

Coping with Sleep Issues Workbook
Facilitator Reproducible Guided Self-Exploration Activities

Printed in the United States of America

Editorial Director: Carlene Sippola
Art Director: Mathew Pawlak

Library of Congress Control Number: 2017940033
ISBN:978-157025-352-2

Introduction to the
Coping with Sleep Issues Workbook

Most people, at one time or another, have experienced trouble falling asleep or staying asleep. Inability to sleep occasionally is normal and is often the result of some sort of stress in life. However, when sleep problems become a regular occurrence and begin to affect one's ability to function in daily life, the person may have developed a sleep disorder.

A lack of adequate sleep may not seem like a big problem, but it can seriously affect one's performance at school or work, ability to concentrate, ability to control emotions, and ability to handle stress. Lack of sleep is a challenge to one's own general health and well-being.

Adequate sleep is a great buffer that helps to protect people from everyday stress. Sleep is a vital support for one's ability to rejuvenate the mind and body.

Any type of sleep deficiency can seriously increase one's vulnerability to a variety of physical disorders and to a host of negative feelings, emotions, and behaviors:

- anger
- anxiety
- frustration
- irrational thinking
- irritability
- sadness

Inadequate sleep:

- a reduction in the **amount** of sleep one experiences. This occurs when people find that they are not sleeping enough hours each night.

- a reduction in the **quality** of sleep one is receiving. This occurs when people find that they are having a hard time falling asleep, often awaken, and then may difficulty going back to sleep. This reduction causes a dramatic break in the sleep cycle.

The *Coping with Sleep Issues Workbook* provides assessments and self-guided activities to help participants learn useful ways to explore, find support, and ways to cope effectively with problems and disorders related to sleep. Many choices of self-exploration activities are provided for participants to determine which best suit their unique needs.

What is the Sleep Cycle?

Sleep is an altered state of consciousness in which brain waves pass through distinct stages that keep cycling between REM (Rapid-Eye Movement) and Non-REM sleep. This is referring to the sleep cycle, and this is how the sleep cycle works:

There are four stages of sleep: Stage 1, Stage 2, Stage 3, and REM. These stages do not always occur in order. In fact, they rarely occur in order.

The sleep cycle begins with three Non-REM phases that people typically go through before reaching REM sleep:

Stage 1 – TRANSITION

This stage between asleep and awake is almost always first. It may be just a minute or so long, but is usually less. It is just a transition from awake to Stage 2 where one spends about seventy-five percent of the night. Typically, a person will drift straight through Stage 1 for a minute or two, and be in Stage 2 for some time. One's eyes are closed, but it's easy to wake the person up.

Stage 2 – LIGHT SLEEP

This is a light sleep. One's heart rate slows and one's body temperature drops. The body is getting ready for deep sleep.

Stage 3 – DEEP SLEEP

This stage is tricky. Deep sleep is also called delta sleep. It is the restorative sleep for the body, when the brain secretes growth hormones, and when our breathing is most regulated. Children have a long period of delta sleep. As we age, the amount of delta sleep that we have decreases by a certain percent each year, so that by the time we reach ages 60 to 70 we have little to NO delta sleep. Men begin to bypass the delta sleep stage sooner than women. So, it is likely that in an adult population, researchers will not see delta when studying a normal night of sleep. There will be a night here and there when an adult will have an instance of some delta activity, but it is not a stage that they go through on a nightly basis.

It is harder to rouse one during this stage, and if someone wakes one up, one would feel disoriented for a few minutes. During the deep stages of Non-REM sleep, the body repairs and re-grows tissues, builds bone and muscle, and strengthens the immune system.

The Sleep Cycle now moves into deep REM sleep:

Usually, REM sleep happens approximately 90 minutes after one falls asleep. The first period of REM typically lasts 10 minutes. Each of the later REM stages gets longer, and the final one may last up to an hour. One's heart rate and breathing quicken. One tends to have dreams during REM sleep. The cycle then begins all over again. The last REM cycle is the longest and most restorative and awakening during this cycle can leave one feeling disoriented.

Format of *Coping with Sleep Issues Workbook*

The *Coping with Sleep Issues Workbook* contains assessments and guided self-exploration activities for a variety of populations to help participants cope more effectively with the effects of viable sleep.

Each chapter of this workbook begins with an annotated Table of Contents with notes and examples for the facilitator. Each chapter contains two primary elements:
1) a set of assessments to help participants gather information about themselves in a focused situation,
2) a set of guided self-exploration activities to help participants process information and learn ways of coping with the sleep issues they are experiencing.

Assessments

Each chapter opens with an assessment that provides participants with valuable information about themselves. These assessments help identify productive and unproductive patterns of behavior and life skills, and guide development of an awareness of ways to interact with the world. Assessments provide a path to self-discovery through participants' exploration of their unique traits and behaviors. The purpose of these assessments is not to categorize people, but to allow them to explore various elements that are critical for success in coping with sleep issues in everyday life. This workbook contains self-assessments and not tests. Traditional tests measure knowledge and elicit either right or wrong responses. For the assessments provided in this workbook, remind participants that there are no right or wrong answers. These assessments ask only for opinions or attitudes about topics related to a variety of coping skills and abilities.

The assessments in this workbook are based on self-reported data. In other words, the accuracy and usefulness of the information is dependent on the information that participants provide honestly about themselves. All of the assessments in this workbook are designed to be administered, scored, and interpreted by the participants as a starting point for them to begin to learn more about themselves and their coping skills. Remind participants that the assessments are exploratory exercises and not a determination of abilities. These assessments are not a substitute for professional assistance. If you feel any of your participants need more assistance than you can provide, please refer them to an appropriate professional.

As your participants begin the assessments in this workbook give these instructions:
- There is no time limit for completing the assessments. You may work at your own pace. Allow yourself time to reflect on your results and how they compare to what you already know about yourself.
- Do not answer the assessments as you think others would like you to answer them or how you think others see you. These assessments are for you to reflect on your life and explore some of the barriers that are keeping you from getting adequate amounts of sleep.
- Assessments are powerful tools, but only if you are honest with yourself. Take your time and be truthful in your responses so that your results are an actual reflection of you. Your level of commitment in completing the assessments honestly will determine how much you learn about yourself.
- Before completing each assessment, be sure to read the instructions. The assessments have similar formats, but they have different scales, responses, scoring instructions and methods for interpretation.
- Finally, remember that learning about yourself should be a positive and motivating experience. Don't stress about taking the assessments or about the discovery of your results. Just respond honestly and learn as much about yourself as you can.

Format of *Coping with Sleep Issues Workbook* (Continued)

Guided Self-Exploration Activities

Guided self-exploration activities assist participants in self-reflection and enhance self-knowledge, identify ongoing and potential ineffective behaviors, and teach more effective ways of coping. Guided self-exploration is designed to help participants make a series of discoveries that lead to increased social and emotional competencies, as well as to serve as an energizing way to help participants grow personally and professionally. These brief, easy-to-use self-reflection tools are designed to promote insight and self-growth.

Many different types of guided self-exploration activities are provided for you to pick and choose the activities most needed by, and most appealing to, your participants.

The unique features of self-guided exploration activities make them usable and appropriate for a variety of individual sessions and group sessions.

Features of Guided Self-Exploration Activities

- **Quick, easy and rewarding to use** – These guided self-exploration activities are designed to be an efficient, appealing method for motivating participants to explore information about themselves - including their thoughts, feelings, and behaviors - in a relatively short period of time.
- **Reproducible** – Because the guided self-exploration activities can be reproduced by the facilitator, no more than the one workbook is needed. You may photocopy as many pages as you wish for your participants. If you want to add or delete words on a page, make one photocopy, white out and/or write your own words, and then make photocopies from your personalized master.
- **Participative** – These guided self-exploration activities help people to focus their attention quickly, aid them in the self-reflection process, and guide them in learning new and more effective ways of coping.
- **Motivating to complete** – The guided self-exploration activities are designed to be an energizing way for participants to engage in self-reflection and learn about themselves. Various activities and modalities are included to enhance the learning process related to developing important social and emotional competency skills.
- **Low risk** – The guided self-exploration activities are designed to be less threatening than formal assessments and structured exercises. They are user-friendly; participants will generally feel more aware and motivated after completing these activities.
- **Adaptable to a variety of populations** – The guided self-exploration activities can be used with many different populations and can be tailored to meet the needs of the specific population with whom you work.
- **Focused** – Each guided self-exploration activity is designed to focus on a single coping issue, thus enhancing the experience for participants.
- **Flexible** – The guided self-exploration activities are flexible and can be used independently or to supplement other types of interventions.

Chapter Elements

The *Coping with Sleep Issues Workbook* is designed to be used either independently or as part of an integrated curriculum. You may administer any of the assessments and the guided self-exploration activities to an individual or a group with whom you are working, or you may administer any of the activities over one or more days. Feel free to pick and choose those assessments and activities that best fit the outcomes you desire.

The first page of each chapter begins with a Table of Contents annotated with ideas and examples for the facilitator.

Assessments – Assessments with scoring directions and interpretation materials begin each chapter. The authors recommend that you begin presenting each topic by asking participants to complete the assessment. Facilitators can choose one or more, or all of the activities relevant to their participants' specific needs and concerns.

Guided Self-Exploration Activities - Practical questions and activities to prompt self-reflection and promote self-understanding are included after each of the assessments. These questions and activities foster introspection and promote pro-social behaviors and coping skills. The activities in this workbook are tied to the assessments so that you can identify and select activities quickly and easily.

The activities are divided into four chapters to help identify and select assessments easily and quickly:

Chapter 1: My Sleep Symptoms
  This chapter helps participants to explore the quality of their sleep along with the symptoms related to their lack of sleep, and determine what may be keeping them from getting adequate amounts of sleep.

Chapter 2: Changes I Can Make
  This chapter helps participants to explore bedroom routines that may prevent sleep and to set up specific accommodations for sleeping more effectively.

Chapter 3: Overcoming Common Causes
  This chapter helps participants to identify the various ways stress, anxiety, and environmental situations can be contributing to a lack of sleep, and to explore ways of overcoming some of these issues.

Chapter 4: Self-Awareness and Self-Care
  This chapter helps participants to explore ways of being aware of their issues and to define ways to take care of themselves by developing effective sleep habits.

Table of Contents

Table of Contents *(continued)*

Our thanks to these professionals who make us look good!

Editorial Director: Carlene Sippola
Art Director: Mathew Pawlak

Reviewers: Carol Butler Cooper, MS Ed, RN, C
Editor and Lifelong Teacher: Eileen Regen, M.Ed., CJE
Proofreader: Jay Leutenberg, CASA

~~~~~~

Special Thanks to
Skylar Park, RPSGT
Registered Polysomnographic Technologist
and a member of the AAST, American Academy of Sleep Technologists

My Sleep Symtoms

Table of Contents and Facilitator Notes

To stimulate interest in the topic, begin each session by asking the suggested questions for the page you will be using.

What disturbance or noise affects your sleep?

Approximately how much time does it usually take for you to fall asleep?

How would you describe your sleep issues?

When do you tend to doze off during the day?

When to you tend to get sleepy, other than bedtime? Do you nap? If so, for how long?

Name ways you have tried to get a better sleep at bedtime.

How many times do you wake up during your bedtime?

(Continued on the next page)

Table of Contents and Facilitator Notes *(Continued)*

 © 2017 WHOLE PERSON ASSOCIATES, 101 WEST 2ND STREET, SUITE 203, DULUTH MN 55802 • 800-247-6789 • WHOLEPERSON.COM

My Sleep Symptoms Scale
Introduction and Directions

Everyone experiences sleeplessness from time to time. When this happens regularly you usually begin to show specific signs of sleep deprivation. These signs point out that you are experiencing sleep problems, or that you may have a sleep disorder.

My Sleep Symptoms Scale contains 20 statements designed to help you explore your current experiences, signs, and symptoms which indicate that you may have a sleep issue.

Read each of the statements and decide whether the statement describes you or not. If the statement does describe you, circle the number in the YES column next to that item. If the statement does not describe you, circle the number in the NO column next to that item. Do not worry about the numbers for now.

In the following example, the circled 2 indicates the statement does describe the person completing the inventory:

                                       YES NO

Because of my lack of sleep...

   1. I am tired most of the time that I am awake . . . .(2)   1

This is not a test. Since there are no right or wrong answers, do not spend too much time thinking about your answers. Be sure to respond to every statement.

(Turn to the next page and begin.)

My Sleep Symptoms Scale

Name _____ Date _____

		YES	NO

Because of my lack of sleep...

		YES	NO
1.	I am tired most of the time that I am awake	2	1
2.	I have difficulty staying awake at work	2	1
3.	I am irritable during the day	2	1
4.	I have trouble concentrating	2	1
5.	I nap at every opportunity that I get	2	1
6.	I have low energy	2	1
7.	I have difficulty falling asleep	2	1
8.	I have trouble going back to sleep once awakened	2	1
9.	I often wake up earlier than I need to	2	1
10.	I do not feel rejuvenated after sleeping	2	1
11.	I am exhausted during the day	2	1
12.	I frequently awaken during the night	2	1
13.	I feel tired when I am driving	2	1
14.	My performance at work is suffering	2	1
15.	I am preoccupied with thoughts about sleeping	2	1
16.	I have tension headaches	2	1
17.	I sleep for only short periods at a time	2	1
18.	I am experiencing increased mishaps and frequent mistakes	2	1
19.	My mind "races" at night	2	1
20.	I am moody, irritable, and/or angry most of the time	2	1

TOTAL = _____

My Sleep Symptoms Scale

Scoring Directions

The *My Sleep Symptoms Scale* you just completed is designed to measure your symptoms from the lack of sleep you may be experiencing. For the scale on the previous page, add up the numbers you circled. Put that total on the line marked TOTAL at the end of the scale.

Then, transfer your total to the space below:

My Sleep Symptoms Total = _____

Profile Interpretation

SCORE	RESULT	INDICATIONS
20 - 26	Low	Low scores indicate that you are experiencing few signs and symptoms of sleep problems.
27 - 33	Moderate	Moderate scores indicate that you are experiencing quite a significant number of signs and symptoms of sleep problems.
34 - 40	High	High scores indicate that you are experiencing a large number of signs and symptoms of sleep problems.

Scale Description

My Sleep Symptoms

People scoring high on this scale are having a difficult time getting to sleep and staying asleep. They often wake up during their sleep time, and then may have difficulty going back to sleep. They experience an inadequate quality and/or quantity of needed sleep. Consequently, they are sleepy within hours of waking up, and their performance at work, school, or in the home may suffer. They often show signs of irritability and low energy.

Disturbances to My Sleep

Often, people who have sleep issues are affected by disturbances and noises that wouldn't affect people who have no problems with sleep. In the space below, write about and describe what disturbes you and how when you are trying to go to sleep, or when you are already asleep.

Have some fun! Draw pictures of those annoying disturbances.

Good Sleep Time vs. Bad Sleep Time

Respond to the following questions to document your hourly sleep patterns.

I have _____ hours of **good** sleep.

This is how it affects me the rest of the day or night. _____

_____

_____

_____

I have _____ hours of **poor or no** sleep.

This is how it affects me the rest of the day or night. _____

_____

_____

_____

When I have **good** sleep, it takes me _____ minutes/hours to fall asleep.

This is how it affects me the rest of the day or night. _____

_____

_____

_____

When I have **poor** sleep, it takes me _____ minutes/hours to fall asleep. Why?

_____

_____

This is how it affects me the rest of the day or night. _____

_____

(Continued on the next page)

Good Sleep Time vs. Bad Sleep Time *(Continued)*

During **good** sleep times, I awaken _____ times.

How quickly do you fall back asleep? _____

_____

_____

_____

During **poor** sleep times, I awaken _____ times.

How quickly do you fall back asleep? _____

_____

_____

_____

During **good** sleep time, I only stay awake for _____ minutes/hours after initially falling asleep.

What helps you fall back asleep?_____

_____

_____

_____

During **poor** sleep time, I only stay awake for ___ minutes/hours after initially falling asleep.

What prevents you from falling back asleep? _____

_____

_____

_____

Which sleep pattern issues do you need to work on the most?

Reflecting on My Lack of Sleep

**By journaling about the sleep problems you experience
you can better recognize the patterns related to your lack of sleep.
Respond to the prompts below and on the next page.**

How long ago did you begin to have sleep issues? _____

How would you describe your sleep issues?

_____

_____

_____

Do you feel tired or sluggish during the day? ☐ Yes or ☐ No

If yes, how often does this happen? _____

Describe how you experience this tiredness and sluggishness:

_____

_____

_____

Do you ever have a problem at work because of sleepiness? ☐ Yes or ☐ No

If yes, how often does this happen? _____

Describe how you experience this problem:

_____

_____

_____

Do you ever have a problem with falling because of sleepiness? ☐ Yes or ☐ No

If yes, how often does this happen? _____

Describe how you experience these falls:

_____

_____

_____

(Continued on the next page)

Reflecting on My Lack of Sleep *(Continued)*

Have you ever had any accidents or near accidents because of sleepiness? ☐ Yes or ☐ No

If yes, how often does this happen? _____

Describe how you experience these accidents or near accidents:

_____

_____

_____

Have you ever fallen asleep without meaning to because of a lack of sleep? ☐ Yes or ☐ No

If yes, how often does this happen? _____

Describe what leads up to your falling asleep:

_____

_____

_____

Describe how your lack of sleep affects your loved ones.

_____

_____

_____

What have you already tried to help resolve your sleep issues?

_____

_____

_____

What would you be willing to try in order to help your sleep issues?

_____

_____

_____

When I am Most Likely to Doze

The following assessment is designed to help you explore those times when you are most likely to doze off. For each of the items, circle the 1, 2, or 3 to describe your situation.

I am most likely to doze off when I am ...

	Not Likely	Somewhat Likely	Very Likely
driving a car	1	2	3
bathing	1	2	3
eating	1	2	3
on the computer	1	2	3
meditating	1	2	3
reading	1	2	3
riding in a car, airplane, train	1	2	3
sitting in a meeting	1	2	3
talking	1	2	3
watching television	1	2	3
at work	1	2	3
other _____	1	2	3

Put an X by the circled numbers 2 or 3 that are not okay for you to doze.

_____

_____

_____

My Sleepy Times

People with sleep issues often feel sleepy during certain times of the day and it affects them in different ways! Complete the table.

Times of the Day	When I Get Sleepy	How It Affects Me	How I am/am not able to do what needs to be done
6 a.m. to 9 a.m.			
9 a.m. to 12 noon			
12 noon to 3 p.m.			
3 p.m. to 6 p.m.			
6 p.m. to 9 p.m.			
9 p.m. to 12 midnight			
12 midnight to 3 a.m.			
3 a.m. to 6 a.m.			

Trying to Get Better Sleep

You have probably attempted many different ways to try to sleep better. This exercise will help you reflect upon and make a record of your various attempts to achieve good sleep.

Identify the various ways you have tried to remedy your sleep problems.

I've Tried This	What I Did	Success? No Success? Why?
Change sleep time and/or nap time		
Changes to the room where I sleep		
Computer games, TV, cell phone, tablet		
Doctor or therapist		
Eating, drinking, substances: a different approach		
Prescriptions or over the counter medicines		
Relaxation techniques		
Other		

Sleep Log

People with sleep issues need to be aware of their sleep patterns over a period of weeks. The log that follows will allow you to track your sleep habits. Within thirty minutes of awakening, complete the log referring to the previous bedtime sleep.

Photocopy this page and do this for two weeks.

Date/Day of Week _____

Before bed, I _____

_____

I went into bed at _____ a.m./p.m.

I turned the lights off at _____ a.m./p.m.

I fell asleep around _____ a.m./p.m.

I awoke about this many times _____

When I woke up, I was awake for approximately _____

To get back to sleep, I _____

My rating for this sleep:

1	2	3	4	5	6	7	8	9	10
Poor				Average					Great

At bedtime tomorrow, I will try _____

_____

_____

_____

Medication Use

It is important to track the medications you take
before you go to bed.

Medications can greatly influence how well you sleep and how
rested you feel after waking up.

Identify the medications you take.

Medications I Take	The Purpose of the Medication	How the Medication Works for Me
Prescriptions for sleep		
Over-the-counter meds		
Other prescriptions not taken for sleep		
Herbal remedies		
Other		

*If you take more than one medication, be sure to check with your
pharmacist to confirm that the various medications are compatible with
each other and check to find out if the medications interfere with sleep.*

Substance Use With or Without Medications

It is important to track your use of various substances that you use before you go to bed especially those along with medications you take.

Mixing substances with medications greatly influence your sleep and how you feel after waking up.

SUBSTANCES	DESCRIBE YOUR USE OF THE SUBSTANCES	MEDICATIONS YOU TAKE	DESCRIBE YOUR SLEEP REACTIONS
Alcohol			
Caffeine			
Illicit drugs			
Legal drugs			
Nicotine			
Over the counter sleeping pills or aids			
Stimulants or energy drinks			
Other			

Often the use of substances is not worth the effects they can have on your body: addiction, withdrawal, or interference with other medications.

Sleep and Mental Health Factors

The presence of one or more mental health issues (and the medications provided to help with the issues) can often cause a lack of sleep. Identify the various types of issues for which you have been treated, the medications provided for you, and their effect on your sleep behavior and patterns. Effects can include such issues as depression, anxiety, mental health disorders, extreme stress, and others.

Treatment Problems	Medications	How The Medications Affect My Sleep

My Lack of Sleep

People who experience many sleepless nights have a variety of feelings about their situation. Use the box below, the reverse side, and/or a poster board to tell your story and explore your feelings with words, drawings, doodles, cut outs from magazines, computer icons, etc. about the experience.

What representation above is most significant to you? Why?

_____

_____

_____

_____

Me ... With a Good Sleep

Think about how you feel and act after a good sleep.
What are you like? How do you act? React? Feel?
Respond to the following sentence starters to get a sense of who you are.

With *a good sleep* ...

I am able to ...

I feel   ...

I accomplish ...

I never ...

My family says I am ...

My friends say I am ...

Is there anything else you notice about yourself after you have had a good sleep?

Me ... Without a Good Sleep

Think about yourself and how you act when you do not get a good sleep.
What are you like? How do you act? React? Feel?
Respond to the following sentence starters to get a sense of who you are..

Without a good sleep ...

I am not able to ...

I feel ...

I fail to accomplish ...

I never ...

My family says I am ...

My friends say I am ...

Is there anything else you notice about yourself after you have NOT had a good sleep?

Quotations about Sleep

Choose one or more of the following quotations and write your thoughts about it.

Control what you can control. Don't lose sleep worrying about things that you don't have control over, because at the end of the day, you still won't have control over them.

~ Cam Newton

_____

_____

_____

Though sleep is called our best friend, it is a friend who often keeps us waiting.

~ Jules Verne

_____

_____

_____

If you have difficulty sleeping or are not getting sleep or sleep of good quality, you need to learn the basics of sleep hygiene, make appropriate changes, and possibly consult a sleep expert.

~ Andrew Weil

_____

_____

_____

Sleep is the best meditation.

~ The Dalai Lama

_____

_____

_____

My father said there are two kinds of people in the world: givers and takers. The takers may eat better, but the givers sleep better.

~ Marlo Thomas

Changes I Can Make

Table of Contents and Facilitator Notes

To stimulate interest in the topic, begin each session by asking the suggested questions for the page you will be using.

Ways to Relax Before Bedtime. .39
What do you do two hours before bedtime?

My Sleep Schedule – Going to Bed. 40
Approximately what time do you go to bed?

My Sleep Schedule – Getting Up. 41
Approximately what time do you wake up?

Napping. 42
How often do you take a nap each day? Each week?

To Nap or Not to Nap? That is the Question!. 43
Talk about any repercussions you might have when taking a nap.

My Bed. 44
Your bed is for intimacy and sleep. What else happens in your bed?

A Tranquil Atmosphere. 45
On a scale of 1 to 5 (5 being the most) how relaxed and tranquil is your bedroom?

(Continued on the next page)

Table of Contents and Facilitator Notes *(Continued)*

 © 2017 WHOLE PERSON ASSOCIATES, 101 WEST 2ND STREET, SUITE 203, DULUTH MN 55802 • 800-247-6789 • WHOLEPERSON.COM

Changes I Can Make Scale
Introduction and Directions

Many times sleep problems are caused by unusual conditions that exist in your sleep schedule, sleep environment, sleep rituals, or activities before you go to sleep. Minor changes in any of these can quickly and easily help you overcome basic problems related to your ability to get adequate sleep.

This assessment contains 28 statements designed to help you explore how you can make minor changes to your sleep habits to begin having enough sleep. Read each of the statements and decide if the statement describes you.

If the statement does describe you, circle the number in the YES column next to that item.

If the statement does not describe you, circle the number in the NO column next to that item.

In the following example, the circled 2 indicates the statement does describe the person completing the inventory:

	YES	NO
My bedtime habits:		
I generally go to bed at the same time..	(2)	1

This is not a test. Since there are no right or wrong answers, do not spend too much time thinking about your answers. Be sure to respond to every statement.

(Turn to the next page and begin.)

Changes I Can Make Scale

Name _____ Date _____

	YES	NO

My bedtime habits:

	YES	NO
I generally go to bed at the same time.	2	1
I generally get up at the same time	2	1
I wait to go to sleep until I am sleepy	2	1
I try to unwind and relax before bedtime	2	1
I avoid too much liquid two hours before bedtime	2	1
I try not to deal with anything too stressful before bedtime	2	1
I try not to watch the clock while trying to go to sleep.	2	1

H. TOTAL = _____

Before I go to bed ...

	YES	NO
I avoid drinking caffeinated or alcoholic beverages	2	1
I avoid sleeping with pets	2	1
I do not eat late meals.	2	1
I do not watch television	2	1
I do not use any electronics	2	1
I engage in quiet activities like reading or listening to soothing music.	2	1
I avoid using products that contain nicotine.	2	1

R. TOTAL = _____

(Continued on the next page)

Changes I Can Make Scale *(Continued)*

	YES	NO

At bedtime …

	YES	NO
My bedroom is quiet.	2	1
My bedroom is dark, with no electronic devices in it.	2	1
My bedroom is a place for sleep (and sex) only	2	1
My bedroom is a comfortable temperature.	2	1
My mattress and pillows are comfortable	2	1
My bedroom is a relaxing place to be in	2	1
My bedroom is free of outside disturbances	2	1

E. TOTAL = _____

Before going to bed …

	YES	NO
I avoid strenuous exercise three to four hours prior	2	1
I quiet my brain with activities like meditation	2	1
I have prepared for the next day so I don't worry	2	1
I have methods for freeing my mind	2	1
I silence my cell phone	2	1
I avoid doing work too close to bedtime	2	1
I avoid taking long naps	2	1

A. TOTAL = _____

Changes I Can Make Scale
Scoring Directions

The assessment you just completed is designed to explore your sleep habits and identify some changes that you can immediately begin to make to help you to sleep better. For each of the sections on the previous pages, add up the numbers you circled. Put that total on the line marked TOTAL at the end of each section. Then, transfer your total to the space below:

H. = HABITS   TOTAL _____
R. = RITUALS   TOTAL _____
E. = ENVIRONMENT   TOTAL _____
A. = ACTIVITIES   TOTAL _____

To get your Grand Total, add your four scores together. _____

Profile Interpretation

SCORE	GRAND TOTAL	RESULT	INDICATIONS
7 to 9 in any single area	28 to 37 for your Grand Total	Low	Low scores indicate that your sleep is being affected in this specific area. You need to make major changes in order to sleep more soundly.
10 to 11 in any single area	38 to 46 for your Grand Total	Moderate	Moderate scores indicate that your sleep is being somewhat affected in this specific area. You need to make some changes in order to sleep more soundly.
12 to 14 in any single area	47 to 56 for your Grand Total	High	High scores indicate that your sleep is not being affected too much in this specific area. You might need to make some minor changes in order to sleep more soundly.

Scale Description

HABITS – People scoring Low on this scale tend to have poor sleep habits at bedtime. They may not have a set schedule for going to sleep and awakening, are unable to relax, and may be clock-watchers.

RITUALS – People scoring Low on this scale tend to have poor sleep rituals. They may allow pets to sleep in their bed, eat meals before going to sleep, and use electronics or watch television in bed.

ENVIRONMENT – People scoring Low on this scale tend to have a poor environment in which to sleep. Their bedroom may be uncomfortable, have outside disturbances, or not be dark enough for good sleep.

ACTIVITES – People scoring Low on this scale tend to be involved in too many activities right before bed. They may be involved in work, talking on the phone, or exercising. These activities make getting to sleep more difficult.

GRAND TOTAL – Low scores on all four scales indicate that the person is greatly affected by a lack of sleep.

The following pages will be helpful to everyone, no matter how they scored.

Ways to Relax Before Bedtime

It is a good idea to shut off your brain before bedtime.
Describe some of the things you do before going to sleep.

_____

_____

_____

_____

Now consider and check off some of the things you might do to relax before going to sleep.

☐ Take a walk

☐ Take a long bubble bath

☐ Play gently with a pet

☐ Meditate

☐ Drink a warm caffeine-free beverage

☐ Watch a calm TV show (not the NEWS)

☐ Breathe deeply

☐ Visualize a positive image

☐ Ask for a massage

☐ Read an inspirational book

☐ Work on a crossword puzzle

☐ Write in a journal

☐ Stretch leisurely

☐ Visit with good friends

☐ Relax your muscles

☐ Listen to tranquil music

Brainstorm suggestions with other people you know.

☐ Other _____

☐ Other _____

☐ Other _____

☐ Other _____

What are the primary differences between how you presently relax before bedtime, and how you might begin to relax before bedtime?

_____

_____

_____

My Sleep Schedule – Going to Bed

It is important for you to maintain a schedule when going to sleep.
By doing so, your body learns the pattern of when it is tired and needs sleep.
In the spaces that follow, track your "Going to Bed" sleep schedule for a week.

Day of the Week	When I Began to Feel Tired	When I Got into Bed to Go to Sleep	Did I fall asleep within a half an hour? Here's what happened.
Monday	_____ a.m./p.m.	_____ a.m./p.m.	
Tuesday	_____ a.m./p.m.	_____ a.m./p.m.	
Wednesday	_____ a.m./p.m.	_____ a.m./p.m.	
Thursday	_____ a.m./p.m.	_____ a.m./p.m.	
Friday	_____ a.m./p.m.	_____ a.m./p.m.	
Saturday	_____ a.m./p.m.	_____ a.m./p.m.	
Sunday	_____ a.m./p.m.	_____ a.m./p.m.	

What is your optimum "going to bed" time? Why?

_____

_____

What is your worst "going to bed" time? Why?

_____

_____

If you can't fall asleep in 20 or 30 minutes, it's time to get out of bed, do something relaxing, and go back to bed when sleepy.

My Sleep Schedule – Getting Up

It is important for you to maintain a schedule when getting up in the morning. Major changes in the times you wake up and get out of bed can causes changes in your rhythm and schedule. This includes weekends and days off work. In the spaces that follow, track your "Getting Up" sleep schedule for a week.

Day of the Week	When I Woke Up Circle *with* or *without*	When I Got Out of Bed And How I Felt
Monday	_____ a.m./p.m. *With or without an alarm clock?*	_____ o'clock
Tuesday	_____ a.m./p.m. *With or without an alarm clock?*	_____ o'clock
Wednesday	_____ a.m./p.m. *With or without an alarm clock?*	_____ o'clock
Thursday	_____ a.m./p.m. *With or without an alarm clock?*	_____ o'clock
Friday	_____ a.m./p.m. *With or without an alarm clock?*	_____ o'clock
Saturday	_____ a.m./p.m. *With or without an alarm clock?*	_____ o'clock
Sunday	_____ a.m./p.m. *With or without an alarm clock?*	_____ o'clock

What is your optimum "getting up" time? Why? _____

_____

What is your worst "getting up" time? Why? _____

_____

The chances are, if you get up the same time every day, even on days off, you will be able to wake up without an alarm

Napping

To sleep well at night, avoid taking frequent naps, too lengthy of naps, or naps for several hours before bedtime. This can throw off your sleep schedule and disrupt your ability to relax at bedtime. Think about each of the days last week.

In the spaces that follow, track your "nap sleep" schedule for a week.

Day of the Week	What I Was Doing When I Felt I Needed a Nap	The Lengths of My Nap	How I Slept At Bedtime
Monday			
Tuesday			
Wednesday			
Thursday			
Friday			
Saturday			
Sunday			

How did your naps affect your bedtime sleep?

_____

_____

_____

To Nap or Not to Nap? That is the Question!

Napping can be a good thing, or not!

See the Pros and the Cons below and note your own experiences.

Pros	Your Experiences
Reduce extreme fatigue.	
Avoid driving or bicycling when tired, or working with machinery.	
Plan a nap when bedtime will be delayed.	
Plan a nap several hours before bedtime, and keep the nap short.	
Improve mood, memory, reaction time, alertness, and performance.	
OTHER:	

Cons	Your Experiences
Napping because of boredom.	
Feel groggy and disoriented after a nap.	
Naps can worsen insomnia.	
Long or frequent naps can interfere with bedtime sleep.	
Naps can worsen quality of bedtime sleep.	
OTHER:	

My Bed

Your bed is for sleep and intimacy only. When you begin to engage in other activities in bed, you are unable to relax and you tend to not associate your bed with sleep.

In the spaces that follow, write about what you do in bed other than sleep or intimacy.

In bed, I do work …

In bed, I play computer games …

In bed, I watch television …

In bed, I connect to social media sites …

In bed, I eat and drink …

In bed, I make phone calls …

In bed, I email …

Other …

A Tranquil Atmosphere

Your bedroom should be a place that is free of gadgets, work, electronics, phone, and anything else that could create stress. It should be a place where you go to escape from all of life's worries and go to sleep.

Is the place where you sleep a relaxing environment with a tranquil atmosphere?

My Bedroom	Yes? or No?	If NO, What Can I Do to Make it Relaxing and Tranquil?	If YES, How I Could Make it Even More So?
It is relaxing?			
It is free of technology?			
Are there no lights or are they dim?			
Is there a lack of clutter?			
Are clocks well hidden?			
Is the room cool?			
Is the bed comfortable?			
Other			

Past & Future

When going to bed, it is often difficult to stay in the present. Negative thoughts creep in about what has happened in the past, or what might be happening in the future. This can keep us awake at night.

Is the place where you sleep a relaxing environment with a tranquil atmosphere?

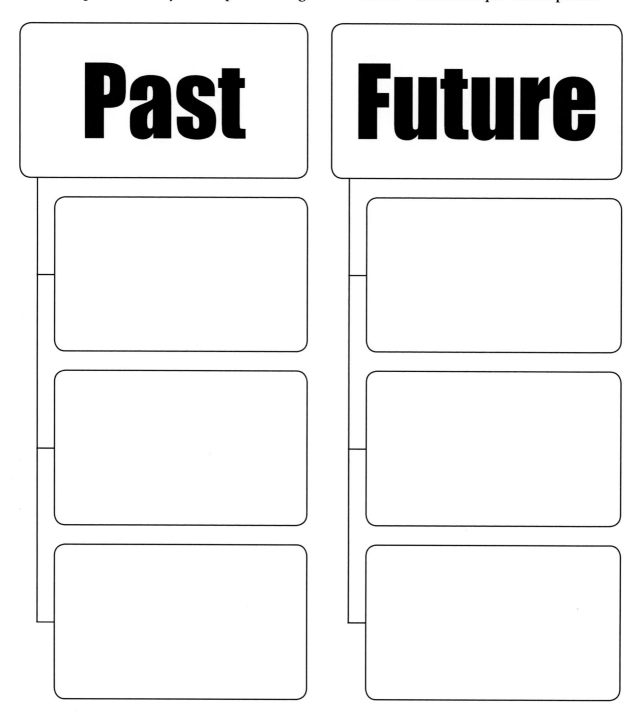

Work hard at NOT thinking about ANY of these things at bedtime!

Quiet, Non-Stimulating Activities

Doodling is an excellent way for you to unleash the power of self-expression. You do not need to be an artist to doodle. You are the only one who needs to know what the doodle represents. Doodling is simply drawing something without thinking a lot about it. It is designed to help you put your left brain (your logical brain) on hold while you use your right brain (the creative part of your brain). Doodles can be silly designs, drawings, abstract shapes, computer icons or simply lines.

In the spaces that follow, doodle four quiet non-stimulating activities you can use to become sleepy.

Doodle 1	Doodle 2
Doodle 3	Doodle 4

Sleeping Better

You can make many different small changes in your sleep habits to enjoy a better night of sleep. Some of these may be more difficult to achieve than others, but many of the ways that you can achieve better sleep at night are listed below.

Put a check (✓) by each one that has been effective for you.

Put a plus (+) after each one that you have not tried but are willing to try.

- ☐ Avoid alcohol, nicotine or caffeine before bedtime
- ☐ Avoid extreme exercises before bedtime
- ☐ Avoid rich foods within two hours of bedtime
- ☐ Avoid spicy foods before bedtime
- ☐ Be sure the bed, mattress, and temperature are comfortable
- ☐ Do easy stretches before bed
- ☐ Do something mildly stimulating after dinner to avoid falling asleep too early
- ☐ Don't watch scary television shows before going to sleep
- ☐ Drink enough fluid at night so as not to wake up thirsty, but not so much that you frequently need to go to the bathroom
- ☐ Eat nothing or something light before bedtime
- ☐ Eliminate loud noises
- ☐ Engage in deep breathing exercises
- ☐ Enjoy a pleasant book on tape
- ☐ Get up at the same time each day
- ☐ Go to sleep at the same time each day
- ☐ Have the same sleep routine on weekends
- ☐ If something is on your mind, write it on a paper next to your bed and then fall asleep

- ☐ If you wake up and can't fall back asleep in 30 minutes, get out of bed until you are tired enough to sleep.
- ☐ Ingest no caffeine after noon time
- ☐ Keep a soft light in the bedroom
- ☐ Keep the bedroom cool
- ☐ Listen to relaxing music
- ☐ Maintain a bedtime routine
- ☐ Make preparations for the next day before going to bed
- ☐ Meditate
- ☐ Nothing in the room but sleep and intimacy
- ☐ Progressive relaxation exercise
- ☐ Read a pleasant book or magazine
- ☐ Save vigorous exercise for during the day
- ☐ Stay away from big meals close to bedtime
- ☐ Take a nap way before bedtime
- ☐ Take a warm bath or shower before bed
- ☐ Take prescribed medications
- ☐ Turn off electronics or technology (other than an alarm clock, turned backwards)
- ☐ Use earplugs to block out noise
- ☐ Use guided imagery
- ☐ Wind down the evening with a favorite hobby, calm music, fun television or book
- ☐ Write in a journal

Relaxing My Mind

As well as preparing your body for sleep, you can also prepare your mind for sleep.
Your mind can be exhausted after a full day of work, family, and friends.
You need to have time for your mind to wind down after a busy day.

To do so, you can try some of the following techniques.
Describe which ones you use, and which ones you might want to use.

I allow myself time to wind down before sleeping by …

I listen to relaxing music such as …

I avoid technology such as …

I avoid watching television by …

I visualize relaxing places or situations such as …

I read a book such as …

Other things I do to relax my mind include …

A Perfect Night's Sleep

How do you envision a perfect night's sleep?
Is it staying asleep all night? Is it getting into a deep sleep that is calm and relaxing?
Is it being pain free all night to allow your body to sleep?
Is it a pleasant dream? No nightmares?
Is it waking up to go to the bathroom and falling back asleep immediately?

In the space that follows, draw or write about your *perfect night's sleep*.

Ask other people what they consider to be *a perfect night's sleep*.

Sleep Myths

**Many myths relate to having a good bedtime sleep.
For each of the myths listed below, write why you agree or disagree with
each myth. Share your answers with others in the group.**

It relaxes people when they play games on a computer before going to sleep.

_____

_____

_____

It's relaxing to do work right up to bedtime to be sure that one is tired.

_____

_____

_____

It is alright to eat and drink right before bed so that one is not hungry during the night.

_____

_____

_____

Having one's pet in bed is always relaxing.

_____

_____

_____

Caffeine will not affect one's ability to sleep well.

_____

_____

_____

Stress has no effect on how well one sleeps.

_____

_____

_____

The Relationship between Stress and Sleep

Worrying about everyday issues and stressful events, or searching for solutions to work, school, family, relationship, and money issues can force your mind to be too active when trying to go to sleep. In the following spaces, describe some of the stressors you are experiencing and how they may be affecting your sleep at night.

Area of My Life	Stressor	How It Affects My Sleep
Family		
Finances		
Home		
Relationships		
Work		
Other		
Other		

Just Relax

One way to ensure that you get good sleep at night is to find ways to relax before going to bed. Some of these ways are listed below. For each one, describe your attempts to integrate it into your normal bedtime routine. Discuss with others some different ways of relaxing and write your favorite in the circle marked "Write One."

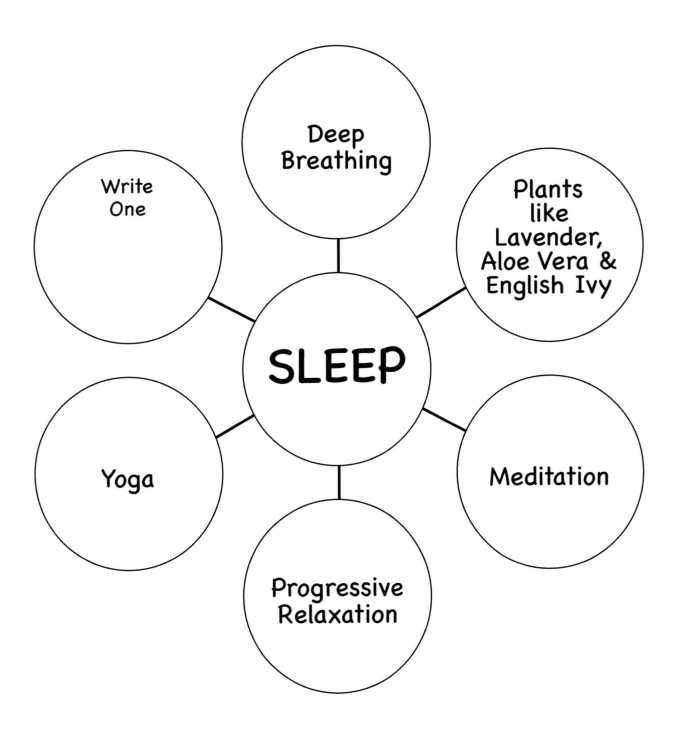

Overcoming Common Causes

Table of Contents and Facilitator Notes

To stimulate interest in the topic, begin each session by asking the suggested questions for the page you will be using.

(Continued on the next page)

Table of Contents and Facilitator Notes (Continued)

Overcoming Common Causes Scale Introduction and Directions

Sleep problems occur for a wide variety of reasons. Many times sleep problems are due to changes in lifestyle, acute short-term pain or chronic pain, feelings of anxiety, or negative emotions.

This assessment contains 24 statements that describe reasons you may not be sleeping well. Read each of the statements and decide whether or not the statement describes you. If the statement does describe you, circle the number under the TRUE column next to that item. If the statement does not describe you, circle the number under the FALSE column next to that item..

In the following example, the circled number under TRUE indicates the statement is descriptive of the person completing the inventory:

	TRUE	FALSE
My sleep is affected by ...		
small aches and pains	(1)	2

This is not a test. Since there are no right or wrong answers, do not spend too much time thinking about your answers. Be sure to respond to every statement.

(Turn to the next page and begin.)

Overcoming Common Causes Scale

Name _____ Date _____

	TRUE	FALSE

My sleep is affected by ...

	TRUE	FALSE
small aches and pains. 1		2
my medical condition. 1		2
chronic pain 1		2
tossing and turning, trying to get comfortable 1		2
pain due to a recent surgery 1		2
pain that will not allow me to find the right sleep position 1		2

P. TOTAL = _____

My sleep is affected by ...

	TRUE	FALSE
working various times of the day or night. 1		2
taking a nap during the day 1		2
staying up late watching television or playing with technology 1		2
taking certain medications or substances 1		2
drinking or eating too much caffeine 1		2
eating right before I go to bed 1		2

L. TOTAL = _____

(Continued on the next page)

Overcoming Common Causes Scale (Continued)

Name _____ Date _____

	TRUE	FALSE

My sleep is affected by …

	TRUE	FALSE
anticipation of something that could possibly happen 1		2
obsessing over work 1		2
watching the clock 1		2
a trauma I recently went through. 1		2
something I am not looking forward to 1		2
worry about family issues 1		2

A. TOTAL = _____

My sleep is affected by …

	TRUE	FALSE
depression 1		2
guilty feelings 1		2
my grief 1		2
a stressful situation coming up 1		2
feelings of anger or frustration 1		2
my fear of something I need to do 1		2

E. TOTAL = _____

Overcoming Common Causes Scale
Scoring Directions

This scale is designed to help you explore certain sleep patterns and habits that may be interfering with your ability to enjoy a good night's sleep. Total the numbers that you circled on each of the four sections. You will get a total in the range from 6 to 12. Then, transfer this total to the space below:

P = PAIN TOTAL _____

L = LIFESTYLE TOTAL _____

A = ANXIETY TOTAL _____

E = EMOTIONS TOTAL _____

Profile Interpretation

SCORE	RESULT	INDICATIONS
6 - 7	Low	Low scores indicate that you have many issues that are keeping you from achieving a good night's sleep.
8 - 10	Moderate	Moderate scores indicate that you have some issues that are keeping you from achieving a good night's.
11 - 12	High	High scores indicate that you have few issues that are keeping you from achieving a good night's sleep.

Scale Description

Pain – People scoring Low on this scale have difficulty sleeping due to discomfort or pain they are experiencing when in bed. This may be short-term or chronic long-term pain.

Lifestyle – People scoring Low on this scale have difficulty sleeping because of lifestyle issues affected by inconsistent work and sleep hours, not enough or too much sleep, etc.

Anxiety – People scoring Low on this scale have difficulty sleeping because they are worried, obsessed about something, and think too much about what they cannot control.

Emotions – People scoring Low on this scale have difficulty sleeping because they are experiencing feelings of guilt, sadness, shame, grief, anger, etc.

Sleep Time Pain

Complete the following rating scales to describe the amount of pain you experience while sleeping.

1) Circle the number that best describes your pain when you first go to sleep.

0	1	2	3	4	5	6	7	8	9	10

No Pain   Excruciating Pain

Describe _____

_____

2) Circle the number that best describes your pain when you awaken during your sleep.

0	1	2	3	4	5	6	7	8	9	10

No Pain   Excruciating Pain

Describe _____

_____

3) Circle the number best describes your pain when you wake up from your sleep.

0	1	2	3	4	5	6	7	8	9	10

No Pain   Excruciating Pain

Describe _____

_____

What can you do, and with whom can you talk, to help you reduce your sleep time pain?

_____

_____

_____

My Pain History

It is helpful to keep track of the onset of your pain, and how it is affecting your sleep. The following questions will assist you in identifying your pain history and its effect on your sleep patterns. If you need more space, turn the paper over and write on the back.

Approximately when did your present pain begin? _____

_____

What happened to cause your pain?_____

_____

What makes it worse? _____

_____

What medications are you taking for pain? _____

_____

How effective are your medications? _____

_____

What pain management have you tried other than medication? (hypnosis, mediation, therapy, etc.) _____

_____

How do you manage the pain? _____

_____

Is your pain constant, or does it come and go?_____

_____

Where is most of your pain located? _____

_____

When do you experience pain? (day time, night time, outside, sitting, etc.)_____

_____

This is important information! Save this paper to take with you to your medical professional. Check with your doctor and pharmacist. Often medications have an effect on sleep patterns.

Connection between Sleep and Life Effectiveness

There is a distinct connection between sleep and life effectiveness. Pain can affect not only your sleep, but your life in many ways. For each of the spaces that follow, describe how pain has affected your sleep, and ultimately affected the various aspects of your life. If you need more space, continue writing on the back of this page.

Because of my pain, I cannot sleep, and then …

at home, I…..

at work, I……

at my volunteer job, I……

with family members, I

with my friends, I….

in my neighborhood and my community, I…..

Which aspects of your life does your pain, thus your lack of sleep, most affect? Explain.

_____

_____

_____

_____

Relieving Pain at Bed Time

People try a variety of ways to reduce the pain they are experiencing in order to sleep better. Which have you tried and how effective have they been? Place a check in front of those that you have done to help relieve the pain. On the line, write the effectiveness of those you have tried or do regularly.

☐ Acupuncture_____

☐ Bed rest_____

☐ Biofeedback _____

☐ Chiropractic_____

☐ Counselor or mental health therapist _____

☐ Exercises _____

☐ Herbal, spice, or essential oil remedies _____

☐ Hot or cold compress _____

☐ Hypnosis _____

☐ Listening to music_____

☐ Massage _____

☐ Meditation _____

☐ Over the counter medications _____

☐ Physical therapy_____

☐ Prescription medications _____

☐ Yoga/Reiki _____

☐ Other _____

What types of pain relievers have been most effective? Which have been least effective?

Most _____

Least _____

Which unchecked items above are you willing to try?

_____

Lifestyle Effects and Changes

It is valuable to think about how your lifestyle may be affecting your ability to sleep well. There are many lifestyle issues that might be keeping you from getting adequate sleep time or that might be keeping you from falling asleep at night. Below, journal about how some of these sleep issues might be keeping you from enjoying a good night's sleep and how you can change your lifestyle.

Sleep Issues	Describe The Situation	How This Affects My Sleep	How I Will Change My Lifestyle
Anxiety			
Drink or eat caffeine products			
Emotional issues			
Go to bed too late			
Late meals or snacks			
Naps			
Computer, phone, games, etc.			
Pain management			
Staying out late			
Work (varied shifts, working at home, etc.)			

Bedtime Steps to Reduce Anxiety

Below is a set of steps that you can use at bedtime to dramatically reduce your feelings of anxiety and begin to effectively cope with them. These steps are designed to help you cope with anxiety from its onset. Think of something you are anxious about, describe it, and then try these six steps to conquer anxiety before bed time.

What are you anxious about? _____

_____

_____

STEP 1 = Reduce physical tension by taking a deep breath and holding it for five seconds. Do this ten more times. How did that feel?

_____

_____

STEP 2 = Stay in the present by bringing your thoughts to the here-and-now (as if the future does not exist!). How did that feel?

_____

_____

STEP 3 = Start the calming process by forming a mental image of a calm place. Close your eyes and picture yourself in this calm place. Use your senses of smell, touch, taste and hearing to make the image real. How did that feel?

_____

_____

STEP 4 = Continue calming your body and achieve a sense of deep relaxation. Start at the bottom of your feet and begin relaxing all of your muscles until you reach the top of your head. How did that feel?

_____

_____

(Continued on the next page)

Bedtime Steps to Reduce Anxiety *(Continued)*

STEP 5 = Realistically assess the accuracy and rationality of your thoughts. STOP any negative statements and replace them with positive statements. How did that feel?

_____

_____

STEP 6 = Repeat several positive affirmations that will help you to stay in the present moment. Affirmations might include statements such as *"My thinking is peace-filled."*

_____

_____

What did you learn from these Bedtime Steps to Reduce Anxiety?

_____

_____

_____

> *The truth is that there is no actual stress or anxiety in the world; it's your thoughts that create these false beliefs. You can't package stress, touch it, or see it. There are only people engaged in stressful thinking.*
>
> ~Wayne Dyer

What does the above quote mean to you?

_____

_____

_____

Activities to Reduce Bedtime Anxiety

There are many ways to reduce anxiety before it spirals into a heightened, debilitating state. These distractions allow you to get out of your own head and focus on things outside of yourself. In each space write about how you engage in the activities.

Physical Exercise Early in the Day (jogging, walking, etc.)	**Enjoyable, Nourishing Activities** (hobbies, family activities, etc.)
Creative Expression (garden, scrapbook, journal, etc.)	**Relaxing Activities** (Yoga, meditation, etc.)

Which of the above are you getting enough of, and which do you need to do more?

Enough _____

More _____

My Negative Thoughts and Feelings

Below, write all of the negative thoughts and feelings you are experiencing today.

How do you think the above negative thoughts and feelings will affect your sleep?

_____

_____

_____

_____

Emotional Pain

Negative thoughts and emotional pain get in the way of a solid bedtime sleep. To relieve emotional pain, you need to deal with it! Explore the various reasons that you are experiencing your emotional pain. *(Example: feeling guilty about something you did or did not do.)*

Complete the following sentence starters to begin dealing with your emotional pain.

Write about something that is on your mind.

_____

_____

Step 1: **Acknowledge your feelings.**

*I feel*_____

_____

Step 2: **Accept what happened.**

Because of _____

_____

Step 3: **Feel it.**

*I will allow myself to feel it by*_____

_____

Step 4: **Don't mask it.**

In the past, I have masked my feelings by _____

_____

Step 5: **Learn from it**

*I have learned the following from my pain:*_____

_____

Step 6: **Overcome it.**

I will overcome my emotional pain by _____

_____

> *Use these six steps when you are emotionally troubled.*

Creative Arts Can Help!

In order to have a peace-filled sleep, it will help to free yourself of negative feelings.

The creative arts can help you in this process!

In the space that follows, create a poem, write a song, create a short story, or draw something that describes what you're feeling and going through.

Try going through this process a few hours before going to sleep.

Regretful Feelings: True or Not True?

It's often hard to know whether feelings about incidents one regrets
are based on truth, or what one believes to be true.

Respond below to evaluate your level of responsibility for what really happened.

The situation you regret and about which you feel guilt, sad, embarrassed, ashamed,
angry, or afraid, is …

_____

_____

_____

Who else was involved? _____

_____

_____

How much control did you have over the situation? _____

_____

_____

Were you really responsible? _____

_____

_____

What could you have done differently? _____

_____

_____

How can you forgive yourself and let it go? _____

_____

_____

Distractions from Dwelling on Mistakes

ALL PEOPLE MAKE MISTAKES!

It's time to move on from the emotional pain of having made a mistake.
Distract yourself from thinking about the mistake by forgetting it and letting it go.

Write about some recreation-time experiences that bring you pleasure.

What activities do you like to do that bring you a sense of deep relaxation?

_____

_____

_____

What activities do you enjoy that bring you a sense of accomplishment?

_____

_____

_____

What activities do you enjoy so much that you actually lose awareness of time?

_____

_____

_____

What activities do you feel passionate about, activities that bring you meaning and a sense of purpose when helping others?

_____

_____

_____

When lying in bed trying to go to sleep,
distract yourself from negative thoughts
by thinking about these activities.

Affirmations

The word affirmation comes from the Latin *affirmare*, originally meaning "to make steady, strengthen." Affirmations help purify our thoughts and restructure the dynamic of our brains so that we truly begin to think anything is possible.

Cut out any of the affirmations that resonate with you and keep them posted in places that you look at it often, on your night stand, mirror, refrigerator, dashboard, etc.

Repeat one affirmation of your choice as you are going to sleep.

I will not struggle. I am peace-filled!	I FORGIVE MYSELF!
I AM SETTING MYSELF FREE.	I choose peace of mind.
I am living in the present.	I connect with the calm of this present moment.
Tomorrow I will enjoy each and every moment.	I am relaxing, clearing my mind, and going to sleep.
MY OWN AFFIRMATION:	**MY OWN AFFIRMATION:**

Self-Awareness and Self-Care

Table of Contents and Facilitator Notes

To stimulate interest in the topic, begin each session by asking the suggested questions for the page you will be using.

(Continued on the next page)

Table of Contents and Facilitator Notes *(Continued)*

Awareness of Sleep Problems and Disorders

Most people, at one time or another, experience trouble falling asleep or staying sleep. Occasionally, not being able to fall or stay asleep is not out of the ordinary; however, when sleep problems become a regular occurrence and begin to affect the ability to function in daily life, it then becomes a problem. A lack of adequate sleep may not seem like a big problem, but it can eventually affect one's ability to concentrate, control emotions, and handle stress. It affects one's general physical health and mental well-being. A sleep problem can easily become a sleep disorder if it is not controlled.

Some Signs and Symptoms of Possible Sleep Problems and/or Disorders

The difference between a sleep problem and a sleep disorder is related to how long the symptoms last. **Sleep problem** symptoms typically have a short-term duration. They are most often caused by a stressor such as a problem at work, an argument, or a medication, and can be resolved easily. **Sleep disorders** symptoms last for a long time and are more serious in nature.

Check off the signs and symptoms that pertain to you and write about them.

☐ Bad dreams _____

_____

☐ Concentration and focus issues _____

_____

☐ Difficulty staying awake _____

_____

☐ Driving when tired _____

_____

☐ Excessive daytime sleepiness _____

_____

☐ Irregular work hours _____

_____

☐ Irritability _____

_____

☐ Low energy during the day _____

_____

☐ Nap soon after wakening _____

_____

☐ Nap more than once a day _____

_____

☐ Nightmares or night terrors. _____

_____

(Continued on the next page)

Awareness of Sleep
Problems and Disorders *(Continued)*

☐ No sense of rejuvenation after a full sleep _____
_____

☐ Not waking up to the alarm _____
_____

☐ Problem staying awake or alert on the job _____
_____

☐ Refusal to get out of bed because of tiredness _____
_____

☐ Relationship issues due to irritability _____
_____

☐ Shift hour change and inability to get used to it _____
_____

☐ Sleepwalk in the house and/or outside of the house _____
_____

☐ Sleepy during most of the day _____
_____

☐ Struggle to fall asleep even though tired _____
_____

☐ Tired or exhausted soon after waking up from bedtime sleep _____
_____

☐ Toss and turn for a long time before falling asleep _____
_____

☐ Trouble getting back to sleep once awakened _____
_____

☐ Regular use of pills or alcohol to fall asleep _____
_____

☐ Wake up too early and unable to fall back asleep _____
_____

☐ Wake frequently throughout sleep time _____
_____

Possible Causes of Sleep Problems or Disorders

The following is a list of SOME of the possible causes of sleep problems or disorders. Check off those you think might be a possible cause of your sleep issues.

- ☐ Acid reflux
- ☐ Allergy
- ☐ Anger
- ☐ Anticipation that something might happen
- ☐ Certain medications
- ☐ Anxiety
- ☐ Bedroom cluttered
- ☐ Caregiving responsibilities
- ☐ Disappointments
- ☐ Disease
- ☐ Electronics (tablet, cell phone, games) in bedroom
- ☐ Emotional stress
- ☐ Family issues
- ☐ Fearfulness
- ☐ Friend relationships
- ☐ Frustration
- ☐ Grief
- ☐ Guilt
- ☐ Hot flashes
- ☐ Hurt feelings
- ☐ Indecisive

- ☐ Isolation
- ☐ Jealousy or envy
- ☐ Job issues
- ☐ Medical issues of self or loved one
- ☐ Mental health issues
- ☐ Overwhelmed
- ☐ Partner
- ☐ Phone use in bedroom
- ☐ Physical ailment or pain
- ☐ Regrets
- ☐ Relatives or in-laws
- ☐ Sadness
- ☐ Social life
- ☐ Stimulants
- ☐ Strangers
- ☐ Substance abuse
- ☐ Suspicions
- ☐ Time constraints
- ☐ Too warm or cool in the bedroom
- ☐ Trauma
- ☐ Uncomfortable bed and/or pillow
- ☐ Worry

Have a discussion with a medical or sleep professional about the items you checked.

Common Types of Sleep Disorders

**Many different types of sleep disorders are listed below.
Check if you think any of them might apply to you.
Then, have a discussion with a medical or sleep professional.**

☐ **Delayed Sleep Phase Disorder** is a disorder in which a person's sleep is delayed by two or more hours beyond the conventional bedtime. This delay in falling asleep causes difficulty in waking up at a desired time.

☐ **Insomnia** is the most common type of sleep disorder. Some of the symptoms of insomnia include difficulty getting to sleep, waking many times during the night, and often waking before it is time to actually get up. Insomnia can affect normal daytime activities. Insomnia is most often caused by stress, anxiety, certain medications, depression and/or inadequate sleep habits.

☐ **Narcolepsy** occurs when people feel excessively sleepy in the daytime. The sleepiness felt with narcolepsy is overwhelming. Some people with narcolepsy have uncontrolled sleepy periods that can occur regardless of what they are doing, while others have constant sleepiness throughout the day. The person has this feeling for a period of time longer than three months, and it is accompanied by a higher than usual percentage of REM sleep.

☐ **Nightmares** are frightening dreams that occur during deep, REM sleep.

☐ **Periodic Limb Movement Disorder** is the movement of hands, arms, feet, and legs during sleep that frequently causes arousals and disturbs the sleep cycles. Whether the person remembers waking or not, the brain often shifts from sleep to wake in a response to the jerking of the limbs causing the sleep cycle to be disrupted and worse excessive daytime sleepiness.

☐ **Restless Leg Syndrome** occurs during wake hours and is often worse in the evenings and before bedtime, which can lead to sleep onset insomnia. This discomfort can come in the form of an urge to move one's legs and feet to get relief. People find themselves experiencing excessive and rhythmic movements while they are sleeping.

☐ **Sleep Apnea** occurs when soft tissue covers the airway, either partially or completely, causing a cessation of breathing for ten seconds or longer repeatedly through the night. This can cause frequent arousals and disruption of the desired sleep cycle. These disruptions cause those suffering from sleep apnea to be very tired during the day.

☐ **Sleep Talking** is a sleep disorder defined as talking during sleep without being aware of it. Sleep talking can involve complicated dialogues or monologues, complete gibberish, or mumbling. The good news is that for most people it is a rare and short-lived occurrence.

☐ **Sleep Terror Disorder** occurs mostly in children, but can be found in adults. Night terrors are frightful images that appear in a person's dreams, but are often difficult to remember upon awakening.

☐ **Sleepwalking** is a disorder that causes people to get out of bed and walk while they are sleeping. It usually happens when a person is going from the deep stage of sleep to a lighter stage, or into the wake state. The sleepwalker can't respond during the event and usually does not remember it.

Sleep Issues

Many people feel that their sleep issues are just a normal part of their everyday life.

Sleep issues can be disruptive and leave one feeling tired and sluggish throughout the day. However, these issues can continue, get worse, and become a sleep disorder.

Identifying and awareness of your sleep issues will help. Things pertaining to your sleep habits that you take for granted may be okay, or they may not be okay.

Take a look at the list on the next three pages, which documents sleep issues. Check the boxes in front of the items that pertain to you and/or your situation, and describe your experiences.

If you know or live with someone with sleep problems, ask the person to fill out the pages, or interview the person by asking the questions, and writing the answers down.

The next three pages, *My Sleep Issues*, will serve as information to take to a medical or sleep professional.

(Turn to the next page and begin.)

My Sleep Issues – Page 1 of 3

Name _____ Date _____

Check the boxes in front of the items below that pertain to
you and/or your situation, and describe your experiences.

While Sleeping ...

☐ I am able to recall a frightening nightmare. _____
_____
_____

☐ I am afraid I will leave the house when I sleepwalk. _____
_____
_____

☐ I am confused upon waking after I sleep walk. _____
_____
_____

☐ I am hard to console when I awaken after sleep walking. _____
_____
_____

☐ I am often sleepy during the day. _____
_____
_____

☐ I am sweaty and my heart is pounding after a bad dream. _____
_____
_____

☐ I dream about doing work while I am sleeping. _____
_____
_____

☐ I awaken out of breath. _____
_____
_____

☐ I am confused if someone wakes me up. _____
_____
_____

☐ I awaken feeling frightened. _____
_____
_____

My Sleep Issues – Page 2 of 3

While Sleeping...

☐ I engage in aggressive behavior. _____
_____
_____

☐ I awaken sweating and breathing fast. _____
_____
_____

☐ I awaken with a dry mouth. _____
_____
_____

☐ I awaken with a sense of panic. _____
_____
_____

☐ I awaken with my heart pounding from fear. _____
_____
_____

☐ I cannot fall back to sleep when I have a nightmare. _____
_____
_____

☐ I do not respond to others when walking in my sleep. _____
_____
_____

☐ I feel scared at the end of my dreams._____
_____
_____

☐ I have difficulty staying asleep. _____
_____
_____

☐ I often choke or gasp during the night. _____
_____
_____

☐ I often have headaches in the morning. _____
_____
_____

My Sleep Issues – Page 3 of 3

While Sleeping...

☐ I scream and shout. _____

_____

_____

☐ I snore loudly. _____

_____

_____

☐ I wake up and sit upright with a look of panic on my face. _____

_____

_____

☐ I walk around while I am sleeping. _____

_____

_____

☐ I will often scream while sleepwalking. _____

_____

_____

☐ My dreams feel like they threaten my safety. _____

_____

_____

☐ My dreams become more disturbing as they unfold. _____

_____

_____

☐ My nightmares are so realistic they are scary. _____

_____

_____

☐ Others say my breathing stops when I am sleeping. _____

_____

_____

Sleep issues can become worse if not treated.

Treatment usually consists of a combination of cognitive-behavioral activities like the ones in this workbook as well as medication. Consult and bring the three pages that you just completed with you to a medical or sleep professional to ensure you are doing everything possible to treat your sleep issues.

My Self-Care Sleep Habits

Sleep habits are often dependent on wellness habits that you display during the day. Think about some of your wellness habits and how they may be negatively affecting your ability to sleep at night. In the chart that follows, write about how you can make positive change in your wellness habits.

Self-Care Habit	My Present Self-Care Habits	How I Can Take Better Care
Example:Eating habits	*I eat a heavy snack an hour before bedtime.*	*I can take a light snack a few hours before bedtime.*
☐ Eating habits		
☐ Consistent bedtime rituals		
☐ Exercise		
☐ Intake of liquid		
☐ Medications/drugs legal or illegal		
☐ Nap during the day		
☐ Relaxation		
☐ Stress		
☐ Other		

In the top left hand corner of each Self-Care Habit, check the habits you can change immediately to ensure healthier sleep.

Exercise for Better Sleep

There is a specific correlation between stress and a lack of sleep. Research has shown that exercise is critical in the reduction of stress. Physical activity earlier in the day can be a key factor in your ability to let go of some of the stress and sleep well.

What types of exercise do you do regularly (jogging, walking, swimming, aerobics, etc.)?

_____

_____

How much time do you spend regularly in the activities above?

_____

_____

Which types of exercise do you like best? Why

_____

_____

Which types of exercise do you like least? Why?

_____

_____

What exercise classes would you like to take?

_____

_____

What stops you from taking those exercise classes?

_____

_____

Are there any team sports that you could join?

_____

_____

Why don't you exercise more? (Be honest!)

_____

_____

How can you compensate or overcome the reasons you do not exercise more?

_____

_____

Nutrition Influences of Sleep

Your food habits may have an influence on the amount and restorative power of the sleep you are currently experiencing. In the spaces that follow, journal about your current food habits, and then identify changes you would be willing to make.

Proteins – *(example: milk, eggs, meat, poultry, fish, dried beans, oats, rice, whole-grain bread, whole-grain pasta, cashews, broccoli, peanuts)*

My current protein habit:

Changes I want to make:

Fats – *(example: butter, cheese, chocolate, pork, bacon, beef, veal, hotdogs, margarine, mayonnaise, canola oil, lunch meats)*

My current fats habit:

Changes I want to make:

Bad carbohydrates – *(example: sugar, corn syrup, sodas, doughnuts, cookies, cakes, pies, sugary cereals)*

My current bad carb habit:

Changes I want to make:

Good carbohydrates – *(example: potatoes, sweet potatoes, fresh fruit, fresh vegetables, corn, oats, wheat, soybeans, black-eyed peas, kidney beans)*

My current good carb habit:

Changes I want to make:

Vitamins – *(example: liver, fresh fruit, fresh vegetables, whole-grain bread, milk, cheese, salmon, tuna, potatoes, poultry, peas, soybeans, whole-grain cereals, seafood, carrots, seeds)*

My current vitamin habit:

Changes I want to make:

Drinks – *(example: water, alcohol, coffee, sweetened fruit juices, sodas, hot tea, iced tea, lemonade)*

My current drink habit:

Changes I Want to Make:

Stress Management for Better Sleep

The relationship between stress and your ability to sleep well has been documented.

People who are experiencing a great deal of stress do not typically sleep well. Place a check mark in the box of the stress management techniques listed below that you will commit to trying.

☐ Avoid *hot-button* topics.

☐ Be assertive with others – you have needs and wants too.

☐ Breathe deeply.

☐ Compromise.

☐ Do not try to control what cannot be controlled.

☐ Eat nutritionally.

☐ Enjoy life's simple pleasures.

☐ Express your feelings in a safe, effective manner.

☐ Focus on the positive.

☐ Forgive yourself and others.

☐ Journal about your feelings associated with stress.

☐ Keep and prioritize a to-do list.

☐ Learn how to say "No" when you feel overwhelmed.

☐ Look at the big picture of life and see where your issue fits in.

☐ Manage your time well so that you have time for yourself.

☐ Meditate.

☐ Plan your time effectively.

☐ Prepare and accept that unexpected problems will arise.

☐ Relax with calming music.

☐ Schedule time for Yoga or stretching exercises.

☐ Spend less time with people who stress you out, if you can.

☐ Take control of your own environment.

Sleep Concerns

People who have sleep problems or disorders often have concerns when retiring for bed because of some of the issues that go along with their sleep patterns.
Going to sleep with these concerns, and worrying about falling asleep, can make it more difficult to fall asleep. Sometimes, talking or writing about the issues will help.

In the spaces that follow identify your concerns associated with your sleep.

MY CONCERN #1

MY CONCERN #2

MY CONCERN #3

Taking Worries and Fear to Bed

We often worry and fear things we cannot control.

Complete this Serenity Prayer, make photocopies of it, and
tape it to your bathroom mirror, by your bedside, or any places
where you can easily see it and re-read it.

God grant me the serenity

*To accept the things
I cannot change;*

*Courage to change
the things I can;*

*And wisdom to
know the difference.*

Bed-Time Self-Care

Cut out the tips below that pertain to you, and those you need to remember.
Post them in places that you will see them. *(bathroom mirror, refrigerator, etc.)*

Reduce your liquid intake before bedtime.	Get at least seven hours of sleep.	Don't go to bed unless you are sleepy.
If you aren't asleep in 20 or 30 minutes, get out of bed until you are tired.	Establish relaxing bedtime rituals.	Make sure that your bedroom is quiet.
Avoid alcohol before bedtime.	Exercise regularly but not three or four hours before bedtime	Avoid caffeine several hours before bedtime.
Refrain from eating a large meal or snack before bedtime.	Remember that your bedroom is for sleep and intimacy only.	Have a bedroom free of and electronic products.
Turn your alarm clock around so that you cannot see it from bed.	Go to sleep and rise at the same time each day – even on weekends.	Keep a comfortable room temperature. Cool, but not cold.
Avoid watching television shows that are upsetting before bedtime.	Maintain a healthy diet.	Think positive thoughts as you are falling asleep.
Consider the things you have to be grateful for as you are going to sleep.	Review the good things that happened during the day as you get undressed.	Free your mind as you get into bed.
Use caution with sleeping pills that can become addictive.	Do not allow cats or dogs in bed with you no matter how much you love them.	If there are noises, use a fan or white noise to block out the sounds.
Avoid stimulants like nicotine and tobacco before bedtime.	Lower the lights a few hours before bedtime	Finish eating anything an hour before bed.
Reduce the number and time of naps during the day.	Make an appointment with a medical professional.	Make an appointment with a sleep professional.

Using Mental Imagery

Mental imagery (or guided imagery) harnesses our brain's natural tendency to create vivid mental representations of our beliefs, desires, experiences and goals. It's also a simple, inexpensive, and powerful tool for soothing symptoms and creating positive change.

The use of mental imagery has been found useful with some sleepwalkers as well as people with other sleep problems.

Mental imagery is using memories of visual events to project a mental picture in your mind.

An example:

> *I picture myself at a beach in Delaware where I used to live. When I begin to feel anxious or stressed I can project myself back to that beach and begin to feel relaxed and sleepy. I just close my eyes and picture myself sitting in the sand. I notice how blue the water looks and how white the waves appear as they come in. I imagine walking along the beach looking for seashells. I smell the fresh air and hear the seagulls chirping above. The sun is warm on my body and I feel safe. With each breath I take I imagine breathing in the beautiful, vivid colors that are present. This is my personal paradise.*

Now, write out a pleasant imagery scene that you will like picturing and remembering. Before going to sleep each evening, you can begin to imagine this scene vividly.

_____

_____

_____

_____

_____

_____

_____

_____

_____

Sweep Out the Shadows!

> *The repose of sleep refreshes only the body. It rarely sets the soul at rest. The repose of the night does not belong to us. It is not the possession of our being. Sleep opens within us an inn for phantoms. In the morning we must sweep out the shadows.*
>
> ~ Gaston Bachelard

How does sleep *refresh* your body?

_____

_____

_____

_____

_____

_____

Which *phantom* does sleep arouse in you?

_____

_____

_____

_____

_____

_____

Sleep Quotations

**Below are two quotes related to sleep.
Journal your thoughts and experiences about each quote.**

The minute anyone is anxious I say: You must eat and you must sleep. They're the two vital elements for a healthy life.

~ Francesca Annis

_____

_____

_____

_____

_____

_____

_____

It is a common experience that a problem difficult at night is resolved in the morning after the committee of sleep has worked on it.

~ John Steinbeck

_____

_____

_____

_____

_____

_____

_____

Support for My Sleep Issues

In overcoming any sort of sleep issue, regardless of how minor or severe, support is important, and sometimes critical. Support can come in many different forms and from many individuals in your life. In the following boxes, list people whom you can rely on to suggest healthy lifestyle changes and activities that allow you to have a healthy bedtime sleep.

Life is not a solo act. It's a huge collaboration, and we all need to assemble around us the people who care about us and support us in times of strife.   ~ Tim Gunn

Possible Supports	Someone Who Can Help Me with My Sleep Issues	How This Person Can Help Me
Medical Professionals		
Sleep Issue Professionals		
Family Members		
Friends		
People in the Community		
People at Work or at a Volunteer Job		
Spiritual Sources		
Other People		

WholePerson

Whole Person Associates is the leading publisher of training resources for professionals who empower people to create and maintain healthy lifestyles. Our creative resources will help you work effectively with your clients in the areas of stress management, wellness promotion, mental health, and life skills.

Please visit us at our web site: **WholePerson.com**. You can check out our entire line of products, place an order, request our print catalog, and sign up for our monthly special notifications.

Whole Person Associates
800-247-6789
Books@WholePerson.com